LOCKED UP BUT NOT BOUND

A Book of Inspirations...
There's One for You

VANESSA A. DOWNEY

Locked Up, But Not Bound:
A Book Of Inspirations, There's One For You

Trade Paperback ISBN: 979-8-218-29978

Copyright © 2023 by Vanessa A. Downey

Published in the United States

Table of Contents

Dedication

This book is dedicated to the Father, the Son, and the Holy Spirit. To the pastors who taught me about ministry. We walked the streets and knocked on doors to pray with people, and to share the good news. Thank you! Dedicated to my husband and daughters, who helped in preparing this book. My grandchildren, who encouraged me. My brothers and sisters, who have supported this process, whether to ask questions or just give a listening ear. Alex, you helped me so much! Thank you!

Introduction

When God told me 10 years ago that I would write a book of inspirations, I put a frown on my face and said I can't write a book! I'm not a writer! The Holy Spirit began to speak through me at my job. When the Holy Spirit spoke to me, I wrote on pieces of paper each night, as I worked the night shift. Over the years, furniture and items were moved around. Those pieces of paper became a distant memory. Years passed, but still no thought of those pieces of paper.

I was doing some home cleaning when I came across a few of those papers. I was in a bit of shock as I began to read them. I thought to myself, *There's more. But where are they?* Weeks went by, and as I was doing more cleaning, I found more and more after that. They seemed to appear. I couldn't believe what I was reading.

I know I wrote it, but some I don't remember. I remembered what God told me 10 years ago. Here I am 10 years later! If God said it, wait for it! It'll surely come to pass. These words are not my own but God's.

*I find myself
being a hugger,
we never know
what someone is
going through.
A hug may
save a life!*

My Love Letter to Jesus

Dear Jesus, You're the love of my life. Without You, I can't breathe. You're every breath that I take. You're the reason that I live. When I was a child with no guidance and direction, You preserved me. I love You for that. You're full of compassion. When my babies were born, You showed me how to be a mother. You have a tender heart. When my oldest daughter Vashonda was daydreaming in first grade, You were a guard to her mind. You made her the smart young woman who she is today. You're an amazing person.

When my daughter Keri had no Pampers and milk, You put people in my life to provide those things. That's why today she has a compassionate heart for those who are less fortunate than she is. I love You for that. While the devil had control over my mind, as I lived in sin, You saw fit to have mercy on my soul. You chose me and saved my life. Thank You for loving me that much.

When I needed to be ministered to, You sent Godly people into my life. They spoke into my life and taught me about ministry. They showed me how to walk in my purpose here on earth. Thank You for that. You're an awesome God! When we didn't have the money for our mortgage, God, You dropped money from the heavens. I love You, God. You're my financial help. When I didn't have a job, God, You put me in a place for a season.

Afterward, You moved me to a better place. You taught me

that we go through things to get to where You want us to be. Thank You for taking me through. You were the fourth person in the lion's den. Thank You for keeping me. When my daughter Bethany had a bike accident, she had faith in You, and You healed her. Because of that, her belief and faith in You is stronger.

I thank You that she knows You at an early age. God, my heart was hardened, but You softened it. I love all my kids and stepkids deeply. I thank You for making me a compassionate person. I love them with my whole heart! God, You deserve the utmost praise. You're greater than anyone can imagine! There is no greater love than Yours. I adore You, and everything that You do! You have performed miracles in my life since before conception.

I thank You that I am a miracle child. Our relationship is compassionate, and our love is genuine! You're my sweetheart, my solid rock, my way out of no way, my doctor, my lawyer, provider, and shelter. You're all that! My Love, continue to be the Almighty Person that You are. Continue to love me and teach me how to live.

Touch and protect the hearts of those around me. Bless my family. Help me to raise our children up in the way that they should go. This is all for now, my Love.

Love You always!

Vanessa

Deliver Me

God, this spirit, called a drug, has a grip on my body and mind. I can no longer think for myself. Sometimes I feel as if I'm losing my mind. I have made this drug bigger than You, God. Even though I know it's not right. I'm finding it hard to concentrate or even sleep at night. I'm trying to hide this thing the best that I can, but God, I know nothing is hidden from You.

I find myself living in darkness; I would love to see the light. I can no longer hide this secret; it's tearing me up inside. God help me to break through this wall to get to the other side. God, deliver me from this thing that has taken over me. I want to live and not die. God, please set me free.

Time for You

I'm so caught up in my job, God. I make no room for You. I'm so double-minded now, I don't know what to do. My family seems to be falling apart, and my house is in disarray. God, please help me find the time to pray to You every day. God, the money that I work for is Yours. Sometimes it's hard for me to realize that. I rarely know where it goes. My pockets have holes in them. Lord, teach me Your ways. Show me how to be the true man of God You intended me to be.

God save me from this life of myself. I put my trust in You now. I surrender. I have no one else to call on. For You said in Your word that You would never leave me nor forsake me. God, turn my life around so I'm no longer fed milk. But feed me the best of meat. I promise You, God, I'll eat. God, my mind is in bondage. Please help me to break through. I promise I'll live for You for the rest of my life.

These Streets

These streets ain't no place for me. There are no rules, no boundaries, no discipline, and no curfews. This is a dark place. There are no lights in these streets, only darkness. My eyes are blinded. I can't see my way. I'm cold and tired. God, I need Your gentle touch. There is no one to turn to in this dark and lonely place. These streets ain't no place for me.

God, You said in Your word that You'd give me shelter in the midst of the storm. God, it is pouring outside, and I barely keep warm. God, Your word says that You're the light. Please lead me out of this darkness. These streets ain't no place for me. I see the light of God: it's illuminating, it's shining bright as can be. I've never seen anything so beautiful as the day God rescued me. Thank You, God.

Put on therefore, as God's elect, holy and beloved, a heart of compassion, kindness, lowliness, meekness, longsuffering (ASV)

The Devil Had a Plan

The devil had a plan for my life. He took my family, my wife. My whole world turned upside down. I couldn't eat, drink, or sleep. The devil had a plan for my life. I was so angry I couldn't think straight. I knew who to call on, but my mouth wouldn't let me speak. The anger rose up inside of me and took over my mind. Even my actions were out of control. The devil had a plan for my life. I felt that guns and drugs were my only friends. They were my protection, my comfort, my way out of no way. One day I hit rock bottom! My whole life flashed before my eyes.

I knew the devil was trying to kill me, as I lay there on the ground. I felt hopeless and friendless. My heart was bound. I tried to speak but the words would not come out. I felt I needed someone more powerful in my heart. Suddenly, a hand reached out to me, as I lay there on the ground. The voice said, "Come my child, take up your pallet, and follow me." On that day as I walked beside that voice, I've never felt so peaceful in my life. My mind has never felt this peace, as I walked beside that comforting voice. I'm no longer bound, but walking in freedom.

The devil no longer had a hold on me. I have the comforter now! He was there beside me in those times when I felt so alone. The devil had a plan for my life, but God had a greater plan!

*Embrace the greatest
commandment, love!
Jesus is love!
Once we embrace Him,
we can love ourselves.*

The Day I Almost Broke

As I wiped tears from my eyes, my mind was in a whirlwind. It seemed as if everything around me was falling apart. I told God, "I won't break down; I trust You. God, I don't know which way to turn, but I trust You. I feel as though my hands are tied and my feet are shackled, but God, I trust You."

My clothes are all torn, my shoes are all worn but, God I trust You.

My finances are low, and my bills are behind, but God, I trust You. From where I stand, I can't see the light, but God, I trust You. This place called home seems to crumble around me but God, I trust You. My mind starts to worry as I try to make ends meet, but God, I still trust You. Don't worry about what to eat, drink, or wear. Our heavenly Father knows what we need (Matthew 6:31). God, You said that You would never leave me, nor forsake me (Hebrew 13:5). I trust You!

13 *forbearing one another, and forgiving each other, if any man have a complaint against any; even as [a]the Lord forgave you, so also do ye:* 14 *and above all these things* put on *love, which is the bond of perfectness.*
(ASV)

I Am Success

Don't look down on me because I'm looking up! When I've done my best with no recognition, I'm looking up! Challenging times and situations come at me like a mighty force of wind. I'm looking up! I am a conqueror. God has poured everything into me to succeed. I won't back down. I am who God says I am. A royal priesthood, a holy nation, a peculiar people (1 Peter 2:9).

I look up because I am success. I'll keep my mind stayed on Thee. I'll remain steadfast and unmovable. I'll look up to where my help comes from. I'll keep my faith in God. I look up because I am success!

*We can't walk forward
while looking back,
an unforgiving heart
will never heal.*

I Am a Miracle

No need to get ready for a miracle. My miracle has already arrived. I am a miracle today. My miracle has already arrived. Oh, God, how I thank You! During my struggles today, God, You made a way out of no way. My miracle has arrived. It was You, God, who quenched my thirst and took away my hunger pain. My miracle has arrived. God, when I was sitting in the sun all alone, it was You shining down on me. My miracle has arrived. God, You sheltered me during the rain and cold. My miracle has arrived. I thank You for that.

Existing today is a miracle. The air that we breathe is a miracle. The water and food that I drink and eat are miracles. My mind is a miracle. My strength is a miracle. God, You stretched Your arms out on that cross. Thank You for loving me that much. You hung Your head and died as You went to hell for me. But, oh, You didn't stay in the grave. On that third day, You got up. My miracle has arrived. If you're waiting for a miracle, He has already arrived.

and be ye kind one to another, tenderhearted, forgiving each other, even as God also in Christ forgave [a]you. (ASV)

I Won't Give Up

I often stare out the window at people walking by, and I think to myself, *Do they really care?* How I long to feel the sun on my face, so peaceful as I close my eyes. I imagine sitting under a tree, enjoying the cool breeze, as the birds and the butterfly fly free. People talking and children laughing. The sound of music, so refreshing to my ears.

But I suddenly realize that I'm not free like the birds in the trees and the butterflies. But still, I won't give up. I can hear the mail slowly approaching. I'm hoping there's an envelope for me. I long to hear from family or friends on the outside. It seems as if they are non-existent.

An encouraging word would be so sweet to my ears. Laughter would be so uplifting. To think that someone even cared would be so hopeful. But still, I won't give up. People go about their lives, never thinking about how lucky they are to be free. The birds and the butterflies are without care of being in bondage; they are flying free.

I can imagine people eating and drinking what they choose. That privilege, I don't have. As I stand and gaze out the window, I can smell the sweet aroma of food. That smell is so familiar, I can almost taste it. My mind wanders back to reality, but still, I won't give up. I wonder what the world has for me now; time waits for no one. I'll keep thinking, wondering, hoping, and praying. But still, I won't give up.

*Never treat people
as if they are
beneath you,
God is above you
looking down.*

Don't Throw It Overboard

Depression has you bound; worry has you down. Unforgiveness keeps lingering; it has a hold on your mind. You feel as if you're sinking, and there's no lifeguard around. When you're feeling anxiety and can't breathe, don't throw it overboard. God is your lifeguard. He has already paid for your depression, worry, unforgiveness, and anxiety. Catch hold of the raft that God has thrown to you. If you keep your eyes on God, you can walk on water.

*14 Wherefore he saith, [a]
Awake, thou that sleepest,
and arise from the dead, and
Christ shall shine upon thee.
15 Look therefore carefully
how ye walk, not as unwise,
but as wise;
(ASV)*

The Son

There is no light without the Son; the earth would be in total darkness. There is no water without the Son; the Son is water of life. The Son illuminates; its light shines throughout the universe. The Son stretched His rays out over that cross on high. The earth shook as darkness covered the Son.

On that third day, the Son rose for warmth, heat, and water. To produce, expand, multiply, flourish, and fertilize. To plant and to shine light on the good roots of the earth that they may sprout up in numbers. I can't look into the Son-light. His rays are too powerful. When I turn and close my eyes, I can feel His warmth and protection. There is only one Son who sits very high. There are some who try to imitate Him, but this Son is our only connection to the power source. One thing I know for sure—we can't live without the Son!

Love
without
ceasing

There's Fight in Me

I'm struggling and can't seem to move my legs. Agony is trying to defeat me. The tears that I cry do not comfort me. The neglect that I feel seems to break me. The world tries to stop me from being all that I can be. But my mind keeps saying, There's a fight in me. Where is the justice in this system? Most are corrupt.

Where are the righteous? Who will defend me in this feeling of defeat? They try to break me down, try to take away my rights. Where can I find trust? Where is the belief system? Yet I still have fight in me. This world can sometimes feel so lonely. People try to block the good for the bad. We must take a stand for the righteous. We must build up, not tear down; encourage, not discourage; love, not hate; embrace, and not push away.

Challenging times are often hard to withstand. The falsely accused need more compassion. Who's our judge? Who will restore my good name? Who will fight in battle for me? Who will stand in front of man to speak life into dark places? The world calls me guilty, but I call myself free. There's a fight in me.

*Know that God is
in the situation with you,
keep the faith, and you
will come out stronger!*

They Gave Me Life

I'm in a different world now. I don't know what it may bring. My life will change forever. They gave me life. I'm going into a place that I have never experienced. Oh, how I long to go back to my comfort place! Fear seems to overtake me, as I begin to cry. Is there peace after the tears? Will I find comfort in a warm blanket? They gave me life.

As I lifted up my head, I heard someone say, "There won't be any rest for a while." The work has just begun. This world that I live in will be different. I won't do the things that I used to do anymore.

The food that I'm accustomed to, I won't taste for a while. While in this room of many lights, and what appear to be many people, my hands are raised up. I feel turned upside down. They gave me life.

People are looking at me with tears. Are they of joy or in a state of surprise? As I'm carried out of the room, I no longer have the same thoughts, I'm no longer surrounded by the warmth and nourishment of a person, but I'm surrounded by the presence of Them who gave me life. As someone once said, it's a mean world out there!

Therefore. take up the full armor of God, that you may be able to resist in the evil day, and having done everything, to stand firm.

If You Never Knew Me

If you never knew me, you wouldn't know that I grew up most of my life without a father. You would never know that my mother was a single parent. There were times when our household didn't have enough food. My mother often went without eating. But you wouldn't know.

My mother often gave her portion of food to her kids. Although she was an alcoholic, she wasn't selfish. Most times we didn't have electricity, running water, or clean water for drinking. If you never knew me, you wouldn't know that I didn't have sufficient clothes, shoes, or a coat to wear during the winter months.

During the summer months, we didn't have air conditioning or a fan to keep cool. Sometimes the heat was unbearable, but you wouldn't know that either, living in a family where alcoholism was the norm. As I think back to those times, nothing about being an alcoholic was normal. People learned how to function and adjust. But if you never knew me, you would not know that.

Being beaten by my father, when everything seemed to go wrong for him, was painful, and depressing. But you wouldn't know; you never saw the scars.

I was talked about, picked on, and bullied in school. Just because, no reason needed. I didn't grow up in a strict family household. There were no rules and no consequences. Either I taught myself, or the streets taught me. If you never knew me, you wouldn't know my struggle. Becoming an adult wasn't as easy as I thought. I didn't know that being an adult came with much responsibility, disrespect, and abuse, mentally, physically, and emotionally.

I was beaten with an extension cord, a belt, a broom, the back of a hand, a fist, pushed down, choked, and kicked. If you never knew me, you wouldn't know that I was afraid to tell. But one day I realized that I was born to be great, the head, above, a conqueror, a leader, brave and not fearful! Get to know me.

Stop Pretending

This face that I wear is only temporary. This smile on my face has secrets behind it. The halo on my head is make-believe. I'm blinging, but it's not real. I've gotta stop pretending. I wear the best clothes and talk to highly educated people. They don't fit me either. Nice cars parked in the driveway, which I sometimes struggle to pay for. My neighbors look up to me. I have got to stop pretending. I don't have much of a college education, but I can talk a good talk and can be very persuasive.

I can mingle with the strong or put on my charm with the weak. I can tell lies and stories to sound so convincing, yet they don't know my story. I've gotta stop pretending. I'm well-groomed every day and highly respected by my family and people who know me, even strangers. But they don't know my struggles. I've gotta stop pretending.

I go to church, clap my hands, sing, and give praise to God, knowing that my heart is far from Him. I feed the hungry, give to the homeless, only to say that I gave. I pray for world change and change in people when my own soul is dying. I've gotta stop pretending. People tell me how well-mannered and educated my children are. But they don't know how I have failed them as a parent.

I wear a fake smile, hold secrets, and act as though I'm an angel. My clothes are cheap, my jewelry is fake. I pretend to be educated to the well-known. My stories sound convincing and easily persuasive. I can talk a good talk, but I can't walk the good walk. I can turn on the charm to convince the strong and the weak to believe. My appearance makes me well respected. I struggle physically, financially, and spiritually. Like so many others, I'm in church on Sundays. I say that I'm saved, but my soul is dying. I've gotta stop pretending.

You Didn't Forget About Me

When You put seed in the ground and brought forth rain, You knew that I would need food. You had me in mind. You created animals and made them good to eat. You thought about me. You brought light and darkness upon the earth. You created the rivers and seas. You knew I needed water to survive. You didn't forget about me. In Your six days of creation, You had me in mind.

While carrying the cross to Calvary, they placed a crown of thorns on Your head, talked about You, spat on You, whipped You, not knowing that one day You would be wearing a king's crown. While enduring the pain, You were thinking about me. When they nailed Your hands and feet to the cross, You shed Your blood for me, died, and went to hell, all because You were thinking about me.

Your body was placed in a tomb, but on that third day You rose up. You didn't forget about me! When I thought I was losing my mind, God, You carried me through and delivered me.

I was drowning in pain and sorrow. You made me walk on water. When I felt that all hope was gone and had no reason to live, You gave me a dream. I was afraid to step out on faith. You took that first step with me. The storm began to rage. You told the water to be still. You didn't forget about me! The enemy tried to come up against me. You stood on the front of enemy lines. You said that You would fight for me. The world tried to take me; the enemy tried to make me. You blocked what the devil thought he had won. You didn't forget about me! I was always on Your mind. As I travel this journey on my purpose, I'm never alone. You won't forget about me!

Can These Dry Bones Live?

A few months prior, my husband poured gasoline on some evergreen plants that became too big to manage during the summer months. As I stood outside my door looking at my plants, I noticed two flower stumps had tiny green leaves growing from them. I thought to myself, *They were meant to live.* People will try to kill what God meant to live.

We have a purpose here on earth, we have dreams, yet people will try to kill them. Our churches have a vision that people won't support; eventually it falls by the wayside. Our teachers have compassion, but no parental involvement. Can these dry bones live?

Our government and leadership have plans, but no one is praying. Our homeless are crying out for help, but our heads are turned. Our elderly are in need of family, but we shut them away and forget. Can these dry bones live? People are being paid less for being overworked, but the rich get richer.

 The winter months and dry summers are harsh on our crops, but we forget who our resource is. There's drought on our land, even in our people, but God is the living water. His words say we will never thirst again. We need to ask ourselves, *Can these dry bones live?*

At times my character is questioned, but I am who God says I am, steadfast and unmovable, a perfect creation from God. God asked in Ezekiel 37:1-14, "Can these dry bones live?" He said to Ezekiel, "Prophesy over these dry bones, and say to them, 'O dry bones, hear the word of the Lord.'" Thus says the Lord God to these dry bones, "Behold, I will cause breath to enter you, and you shall live. And I will lay sinews [tough fibrous tissue] upon you, and will cause flesh to come upon you, and will cover you with skin, and put breath in you, and you shall live. And you shall know that I am the Lord."

Just like the flower stump in my yard, God meant for it to live. We need to prophesy over our purpose, dreams, visions, government, and churches. That plant may look dead on the outside, but deep down on the inside of that root, there is life! Start getting involved, start praying for our leaders, and stop turning our heads to the homeless and elderly.

Even though there's drought in the land, know that God is our water supply. Prophesy to your dry bones and speak life. Watch those tiny green leaves spring up from the root. God said He would put breath in you, and you shall live! Your purpose shall live; your dreams and vision shall live! Can these dry bones live!

He Gave His Best

When God created Jesus, He gave His best. When He sent His Son Jesus to carry the cross to Calvary, He sent His best! God sent His son Jesus to die so that we may live. He sent His best! Lazarus died and was in the tomb for four days. God sent Jesus to tell Lazarus to come forth out of the grave. He sent His best! Great multitudes came to Jesus, the lame, crippled, blind, and dumb. Many others were laid at his feet. Jesus healed them (Matthew 15: 29-31). He gave His best! Jesus fed a multitude of 5000 with seven loaves of bread, and three small fish. He gave His best! A great storm arose in the sea.

The disciples were afraid they would perish. Jesus arose and rebuked the winds and the sea, and it became perfectly calm. The winds and the sea obeyed Him. He gave His best! A woman who had a hemorrhage for twelve long years was healed by touching the fringe of His cloak (Luke 8:43). He gave His best! A certain man in Jerusalem had been thirty-eight years in his sickness and was healed (John 5:1-9). He gave His best! Jesus applied clay to the eyes of a man blind since birth. He said, "Go, wash in the pool of Siloam." And so, he went away and washed. He came back with eyesight (John 9: 1-7). He gave His best! Jesus performed many miracles.

As of today, He is still performing miracles. Bring people back to life, healing, delivering, setting free, and being a comforter to the brokenhearted. Caring for the homeless and being a father to the fatherless. He gave His best! "And behold, a voice out of the heavens, saying, 'This is my beloved Son, in whom I am well-pleased'" (Matthew 3:17).

I Never Would Have Thought

I never would have thought that I would be rocking this short hairstyle. I've always loved my soft, shoulder-length hair. Never would I have thought that I would be involved in a car accident, and my long soft hair would have to be shaved off before surgery. I never thought I would love myself so much with the scar on my face and short hair that I am forced to wear. I love myself some me! God changed my appearance, but the blood that He shed still flows through my veins.

I never would have thought that God would clean me up so well and call me His own. I have never felt so loved before that day that God chose me. Although the world thought of me as a nobody, to God I have always been somebody. I never would have thought! A lady who was very close to me said that if I am blessed, I'm already highly favored. I never would have thought that being highly favored would take me through some ups and downs, heartache, pain, storms, and crisis.

I never would have thought that I would feel so alone while walking this Christian life. But God is with me at all times. He said, "I will never leave you nor forsake you." I never would have thought the footsteps beside me belong to God. I never would have thought that I would help a stranger, give to the homeless, pray for the sick, and encourage the hopeless. I never would have thought that God would one day use me to write His book. But He thought!

Stand firm therefore, having girded your loins with truth, and having put on the breastplate of righteousness.

Our Leaders

Our leaders hold the world on their shoulders; they make tough decisions and endure sleepless nights. Who's praying?

No one is ever satisfied; we draw our own conclusions. We point fingers, place blame. Who's praying? Some leaders make right decisions, some wrong, but still, who's praying? Leaders who keep watch over our souls spend tireless nights crying out to God, yet we won't support the vision.

They have the weight of the church on their backs, yet we try to crush what God has anointed. We look to our leaders in times of crisis, but we don't follow guidelines. We create strife among ourselves. Who's praying? Our leaders put provisions in place, yet we break all the rules. We are so quick to judge while ignoring the fact that God is the only judge. Who's praying?

and having shod your feet with the preparation of the gospel of peace

I Tried to Fight My Own Battle

The Bible says, "I can do all things through Christ who strengthens me" (Philippians 4:13). Notice that it says, "Through Christ." As I was thinking of a certain situation, God reminded me that this battle is not yours. Often, we try to fight battles with our own natural mind, sometimes with our hands. In the end, we lose. We try to fight our addictions on our own. Once again, we fail.

Our demons convince us that we have it all under control. In the end, they come back stronger. God's word clearly says, "Through Christ who strengthens me." I once heard God say, "Keep your eyes on me; you can walk on water. Our own natural mind tells us to start walking, and we sink.

 Our weak minds cause people to persuade us that it's all about them when in the end, they deceive us. Because of the devil's deception, we sink deeper into depression, addiction, anxiety, loneliness, and mental instability.

The Bible says that it is through Christ who strengthens us. We try to fight our own battles, but in the end, we lose. God's arms are wide open, waiting to receive us. He's saying to me, "Child, this battle is not yours. It belongs to Me.

in addition to all,
taking up the shield of
faith with which you will
be able to extinguish all
the flaming missiles
of the evil one.

What Will I Say?

At a job where I worked for many years, people would walk past me and not speak, even put their heads down. I have to admit, it bothered me. I was reminded of God saying, "Every knee shall bow before Him." With that being said, everyone will stand before God. Whether we are black, white, rich, poor, man, woman, supervisor, manager, president, saved, or unsaved. God is no respecter of persons (Romans 2:11).

When God sends people to knock on our doors to share the good news that Jesus saves, will we say, "God, I didn't know?" He sent pastors and teachers to preach His word. Will we say, "I wasn't taught?" The homeless reach out for food, yet we ignore them. What will we say? We build our own idols and worship them. What will we say?

We forget about our brothers and sisters behind prison bars. We think we are better than they are because we sin differently. What will we say? We think we are better than the door keeper and the janitor. Yet they are the humble ones. What will we say?

We cling to the pleasures of the world, yet we forget about who created the universe. Or is it that we just didn't believe?

And take up the helmet of salvation, and the sword of the spirit, which is the word of God.

Water It

On the day of my wedding, The pastor told my husband and me that if our marriage starts to wither, water it! As we know, without water nothing can live. Without God we die. His word says that He is the living water; without this water, we die spiritually. When we die a spiritual death, we are separated from God. While drinking a glass of water, our thirst is quenched. God's word says that if we drink the water that He offers, we will never thirst again. When we are living our lives out of control, water it!

The addiction that we try so hard to break—water it! Our peace and joy are withering. Water it! God said to train up a child in the way that they should go, but instead, they go the opposite direction. Water it! Our dreams, and visions seem to fall by the wayside. Water it!

The wicked ways of the world weigh us down causing us to fall. Water it! In difficult times, we fight to stay alive, stay healthy, keep jobs, and even struggle in our finances and social lives. Water it! They say the grass is greener on the other side, but without water, there is no life. If your grass is withered, water it! And watch your life flourish!

This book is inspired by the Holy Spirit. All the glory and honor belong to God. I am a vessel used by God to inspire His people. He died and came back so that we may live. There is no greater love than God's. It is my greatest hope that this book will lift you up, break chains, deliver, set free, and encourage.

My series of inspirational books is currently in the works. God already has me writing, and I can't wait to share with you!

Leave a Review

If you found this book to be a blessing to you, please leave a review on Amazon.

About the Author

I reside in Braselton, Georgia, where I live with my husband. Together we have five children and several grandchildren. I am who God says I am! A country girl from Reform, Alabama. One of seven children. The daughter of the late Sherman and Gracie Neal Randolph. Also raised by the late Miss Aurelia S. Randolph. Aurelia taught me how to love myself, show respect, give respect, and strive for the best in life. I don't wear things that don't fit me. David said, This garment doesn't fit me; it's too big. There are people who don't fit me, conversations that don't fit me, and garments that don't fit me! I am who I am! The doorkeeper, the janitor, the cook, the prisoner, the homeless. I am no greater than but equal. If someday you shall meet me, I am who I am. I'm just me! Genuine, loving, compassionate, and encouraging.

For inquiries, please email Vanessabinspired@gmail.com.